Ferry Beach

Barrow-in-Furness

A recollection of boatmen, fishermen and their craft

Stan Henderson

Published in 2023 by Stan Henderson

© Copyright Stan Henderson

ISBN: 978-1-913898-73-1

Book & Cover Design by Russell Holden

www.pixeltweakspublications.com

Photographs supplied by the author/publisher Stan Henderson and their sources referenced accordingly throughout the book. Every attempt has been made to contact copyright holders of material in this book where it was deemed necessary. However, if an omission has occurred future editions will include acknowledgments

A Catalogue record for this book is available from the British Library.

Printed by IngramSpark

All rights reserved without limiting the rights under copyright reserved above, no parts of this publication may be reproduced, stored in or introduced into a retrieval system, or transmitted in any form, or by any means (electronic, mechanical, photocopying, recording or otherwise) without the prior written permission of Stan Henderson, the copyright owner and the publisher of this book

"I must go down to the sea again, for the call of the running tide"

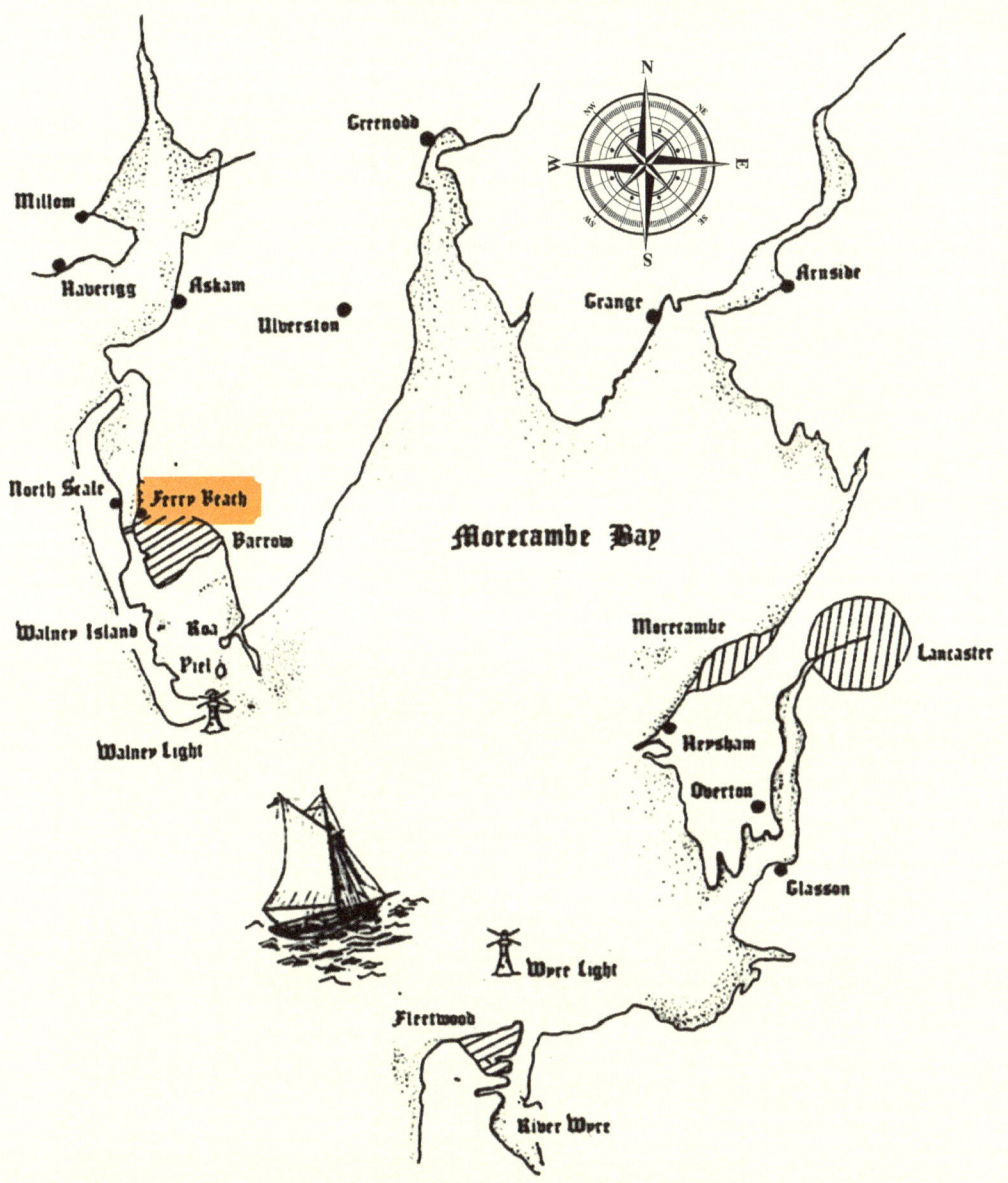

Map of the Morecambe Bay area showing the location of Ferry Beach.
Reproduced from 'Morecambe Bay', by Alan Lockett

Foreword and Acknowledgements

This book started life as a *memoir* and is taken from my family history, which I started to compile in 1992. It is born out of the many enjoyable hours spent on Ferry Beach, Barrow-in-Furness, during the ten years up to 1963.

I think my interest was ignited initially around 1953 when, as a 4 year-old, my mother took me to meet my father as he returned from a fishing trip. Dad came ashore carrying two massive skate (one in each hand). Holding them at shoulder height, their tails trailed the sandy beach. In addition to what could be harvested from the sea, I found that I could spend all day simply looking at and admiring boats – whether they be cabin cruisers, Morecambe Bay prawners or yachts.

For a decade Ferry Beach was almost my second home. If it was raining I would sit in Nicky's hut, along with Jimmy Hollywell and a man called Ziggy. Nicky (Cecil Nicholas) was a full-time (in-shore) fisherman and his shed was the first one situated on the pitching as you turned the corner from Ferry Beach Road. Mr Nicholas was somewhat of a loner. He lived on Earle Street, Barrow Island and he led a very simple life as a single man. He never drank nor smoked. Occasionally he would attend Craven Park to watch Barrow *RLFC*. As well as being a fisherman he was a first-class boat builder. During the period being recalled he was building a boat, *Daisy*. It would be his second with this name (see also Appendix).

In writing this book I have tried to include as many as possible of the characters encountered who, between them, made Ferry Beach such a place of fascination.

Jimmy Hollywell became a friend and a kind of mentor. He taught me how to fillet fish and how to tie a variety of knots (Bowline; Clove Hitch and Half Hitch). Later, when I left school and started work, Jimmy was the first person I worked with (Steel Works). Jim and his wife lived on Stanley Road, Barrow Island.

Other likeminded lads I encountered 'down the beach' were Bob Day; Jimmy Morgan; Joe Murphy; David and Tony Thompson and Brian Warriner.

Because of a paucity of images from the period, some later photos are used where deemed to be typical.

People who contributed to this work and without whose help the project would not have taken off are: Mavis Barnard; Leasil Burrow; Margaret Burrow MBE; Andrew Clark; Graham Cubbin (Dock Museum); Sharon Galloway (Barrow Sailing Club); Neal Henderson; Raymond Hewson; Steve Lawson and Norman Pascoe.

A special thank you is extended to Andrew Clark and Brian Moxham for sharing their collection of photos.

Susan Benson and her colleague Selena Kendal of Cumbria Archives and Local Studies Centre (Barrow), as always, have been most informative and helpful, especially with the sourcing images.

Finally, a special thank you to Russell Holden of Pixel Tweaks Publications for producing the book.

Contents

Foreword and Acknowledgements iii

1 Origins 1

2 Barrow Sailing Club 5

3 Down the Beach 8

4 The Boats 19

Afterword 43

Sources 45

Appendix 47

About the Author 57

1

Origins

Ferry me across the water, do, boatman, do...

Ferry Beach is situated towards the northern tip of Barrow Island at a place called Crow Nest Point. It was named for the steam ferry that operated from this location and which transported people and goods to and from Walney Island.

Access is *via* Ferry Beach Road (originally an un-named lane), which branches off North Road (Low Road) and lies between what was once Vickers' North West Yard and a cluster of allotment gardens. A signal box was situated at this junction. The 'road' was always very coarse and stony and replete with potholes.

Low Road with a motor car at the entrance to Ferry Beach Access Lane. Walney Ferry Signal box stands at the junction. *Courtesy of Michael Andrews (MAA42). G. Holme archive*

If you wanted to cross Walney Channel prior to 1878, you needed to avail yourself of the services of a ferryman (Anthony Strong of North Scale, a champion oarsman of the day, would row you across for one halfpenny). A few years later a Mr Jackson also provided the service. Alternatively you could cross at low tide by way of one of several ancient fords.

An early postcard depicting Ferry beach, the towns' (once) main industry is in the background

A Chain ferry service (No 1), designed by Furness Railway engineer, William Frank Pettigrew, became established in 1878. This was later replaced in 1903 by a different design (No 2). This facility at Ferry Beach included a ramp, a wooden ticket office and also a waiting room, which was also of timber construction. The service continued for almost 30-years before being replaced by Walney Toll Bridge (1908).

Steam Ferry at the Walney Landing, c. 1910. The new Walney Bridge provides the back drop.
Courtesy of Cumbria Archives and Local Study Centre (Barrow).

The first vessel to pass through the new Walney Bridge. (1908).
Courtesy of Cumbria Archives and Local Study Centre (Barrow).

Manx Steamer passing through the Bridge, c. 1910. *W. Pears*
Courtesy of Cumbria Archives and Local Study Centre (Barrow).

Many years later the ticket office was dismantled and removed to the Windermere Steamboat Museum.

Charles Turner was born at Hull in 1899. He was brought to Barrow as an infant during the early years of the 20th Century when his family settled in one of the new houses on Buller Street, Vickerstown. In a *memoir* he noted that:

> *A new Ferry was put on at this time with much pomp and ceremony. It was to be the last as the new bridge had been started. The celebration for the Ferry included regatta rowing races, duck hunt, greasy pole, swimming and diving. All regattas in those days started from the Bankfield Hotel at North Scale, so as not to get mixed up with the Ferry chains.*
>
> *I also recall being taken onto French Street to a position where I could see clear across James Dunn Park and the firework display, also the burning of a model of the Ferry, marking the start of work on the new bridge.*

(Charles Turner, a memoir, courtesy of Leasil Burrow)

2

Barrow Sailing Club

It's a warm wind the west wind, full of bird's cries...

A Royal Barrow Yacht Club existed from 1871, with an Admiralty Warrant granted in 1872. In 1893 the Duke of Buccleuch was the Commodore.

Barrow Sailing Club was formed in 1906 by a group of people who were originally members of the Barrow Yacht Club. This was during the time that Walney Bridge was being constructed. Members started using Ferry Beach and they rented the wooden waiting room of the steam ferry as a clubhouse. In 1919 the Furness Railway Company gave the tenancy of the waiting room, ticket office and also the ramp to the club.

The Wooden Clubhouse, *Breeze* is on the beach (left). *Courtesy Andrew Clark.*

A Commodore during the 1950s and 60s was George Hall, a local undertaker. George's yacht, the *Dairy Maid,* was moored on the Walney side of the Channel and opposite to the Nautical Club. She was a fine craft of marine ply construction. Her hull was always painted sky blue with cream topsides.

Another club member was Fred Rollinson*, a time-served shipwright. Fred's yacht, the *White Rose,* was the oldest and probably the fastest yacht on the Channel. She had been built by the Ashburners, local boat and shipbuilders, around 1887 and had several owners (including the previously mentioned Mr Strong) before Fred. She would regularly compete in the midnight Isle of Man races. As this book is being prepared, *White Rose* is in retirement in Barrow's Dock Museum.

The sleek and graceful White Rose under sale.
Reproduced from Alan Locket's 'Morecambe Bay'.

---

*Fred Rollinson was also associated with a boat called *Red Rose,* of which I have no information: Author.

The sloop Breeze, a very eye-catching form, at her mooring in the Channel.
She was originally powered by a 2-cylinder Stuart Turner petrol engines (2 stroke). This was later replaced with a single-cylinder horizontal diesel (Yanmar).
Courtesy of Andrew Clark.

Barrow Sailing Club members Sam Rowe (left) and George Harper on Ferry Beach in October, 1998.
George had been an apprentice training (Joinery) instructor at Vickers Shipyard.
Andrew Clark collection.

3

Down the Beach

Over my toes goes the soft sea wash. . . .

The Ferry Beach community, during the period covered in this book, was split into two factions, the Barrow Sailing Club membership and the individual mariners. Unlike the present time, it wasn't necessary to be a BSC member to use Ferry Beach. Notwithstanding, both parties were subject to the rules and regulations of the Port Authority. The Channel, north of the Bridge at that time, included the fairway as vessels were still using the Graving Dock. I recall the Manx steamers being laid up there. The last Vickers-built ship to be outfitted in the graving dock was probably? *HMS Mohawk,* a Tribal-Class frigate for the Royal Navy, which was completed in 1963.

  If your boat dragged its mooring into the fairway, the Port Authority were quick off the mark and you were contacted *via* the club. The Authorities did not deal with individual boat owners.

The first character my father introduced me to during the early 1950s was **Hughie Fairbridge.** On the day in question, Mr Fairbridge was rowing ashore in his 'well maintained,' white, 12-foot punt and dad needed to speak to him about our boat colliding with one of the Bridge's dolphins which Hughie had witnessed. Three of the *Falcon's* co-owners had taken her across the Bay to Fleetwood for a few days. At the time Fleetwood was the UK's main, deep-sea, fishing port on the west coast and the only UK port to have three lighthouses! It had been the number one port for Hake - it boasted the best fish and chips - had good pubs and was the home base of the trawler fleet that fished the North Atlantic. Mainly because of the Icelandic Cod Wars, Fleetwood's deep-sea fishing industry disappeared towards the late 1960s. [Successive governments have done little over the years to protect our fishing industry].

Up until 1962 the Isle of Man Steam Packet Company provided a seasonal ferry service between Fleetwood and Douglas.

On the day of their planned return, a gale warning was issued for the Irish Sea and locals advised them to defer sailing. The foolhardy three set off regardless. They departed the Wyre Channel in a heavy swell and crossed the Bay in a force 8 with a beam sea! They had almost reached the safety of home but, because of the state of tide, had to *toot* for Jubilee Bridge to be lifted. It was while waiting for the Bridge that the boat was caught by a sudden squall and blown against one of the dolphins, smashing the vessel's stem and almost demolishing the wheelhouse. (Given the wind conditions it is obvious they should have kept well clear until the Bridge lifted). I think the experience was sufficient to convince the trio that enough was enough. I don't recall seeing them again on any of our, later, fishing trips!

Mr Fairbridge was a slim, well preserved, elderly man with a strong white 'tash. He had a full head of white hair, kept in place under a flat cap. What caught my attention, when he spoke, was his deep, resonant voice. Hugh, at the time of my introduction, lived at 7 Cameron Street**, Barrow Island with his wife and son. It would be decades later that I discovered how remarkable this old gent was.

In 1951, the *Barrow News,* covering Ambleside Sports, noted that the oldest competitor was from Barrow.

> *" 70 Year-old Barrovian in Sprint": The 2000 early arrivals at Rydal Park for Ambleside Sports on Thusrsday saw a plucky effort from 70-years old, white haired, Hugh Fairbridge of Cameron Street, Barrow, who finished second, off 33 yards, in one of the men's 100-yards handicap heats, to J. Ward of Bridgefoot.*
>
> *'I never train to keep fit', said Hugh after his heat, 'because it might make me stiff, but I do a lot of rowing and punting on Walney Channel'.*

** Cameron Street: Originally *Mast Street.*

Hugh was born in Sunderland in 1881. After coming to Barrow he had worked as a shipyard labourer. He passed away in 1972 at the age of 91.

John William (Bill) Thompson lived on Tay Street in the Hindpool Scotch Buildings, following his return from overseas where he had seen active service in Burma. Bill was not time-served but had a natural flair for working with wood. He was, in effect, a self-taught ship's carpenter. During the time that I knew him he was working as a blacksmith's striker in the shipyard. This was after he joined the crew of dad's boat, having recently sold his own boat, *Tony*, a 28-foot converted lifeboat. *Tony* was powered by a car engine (Bullnose Morris if memory serves). Bill always cursed it, saying it was always a 'pig' to start (hand-crank). Bill's hut was one of three that were located on the pier-head, near to the Steps.

There was also a hutment along the Ferry pitching (officially referred to as boat stores). Ours was the third one along from Nicky's (No 19 and which still stands). When dad sold ours in 1963, a man called Conway took it on.

Upon joining the crew of the *Falcon*, Bill set about renewing some of the boat's topsides. All in all he fitted a new afterdeck, together with timber-heads, as well as a new wheelhouse top. He also renewed the entire gunwale and belting in (steam bent) Oregon Pine. All this

Crew of the *Tony*: Bill Thompson (left) and Jack Stockton (right), at Morecambe around 1959.
S Henderson collection.

work was achieved using hand-tools as there were no power points 'down the beach'.

As with many of the Ferry Beach lads, Bill and Jack were regulars at the *Crow Nest* pub. The '*Crow*' is located on the corner of Ferry Road and Stanley Road, Barrow Island and was originally a Thompson House. It was named, not for anything nautical, but from the land (fields) that surrounded it *viz*: Crow Nest; Near Crow Nest and Middle Crow Nest.

The *Crow Nest Hotel* opened in May 1888 and was described in the *Barrow News* as one of the best appointed hotels in Barrow. In August, 1892 the local press reported that:

Edward Wilson a popular landlord of the Crow Nest Hotel, patronised then, as now, by the fishing and yachting fraternity of Ferry Beach, was drowned. Together with Mr R. Tyson of the Ship Hotel and another friend he set off for Morecambe at 9.30 am and arrived about 12 noon. Returning later to Barrow the weather had changed, then a S.W. gale sprang up. They reefed the mainsail and foresail and set a storm jib. Wilson was thrown overboard by a big wave and he attempted to swim. They put the boat out, but were unable to reach him in time and he drowned. They gave up in despair and returned to Morecambe and reported the accident to the police. Edward Wilson was 32-years old. His father and two other men were drowned 29-years previously in a similar incident. As a sign of respect, most local yachts and fishing boats flew their flags at half-mast.

(Reproduced from *Shipwreck and Boating Accidents of Barrow and District* by Tony Diamond).

The *Crow Nest Hotel* with Stanley Road to the left. *The Sankey Family Photographic Collection courtesy of Cumbria Archives.*

The bar of the *Crow* was known as the Fisherman's Bar during the 50s and 60s and you could always be sure of selling your catch there. Years later, for some unknown reason, the word *Crow* became pluralised? Other local public houses where you could easily sell/buy fish were *The Ferry Hotel*, Promenade, Walney Island and the *Wheatsheaf Inn,* Hindpool Road.

* * *

The Brown brothers, of Devonshire Buildings, Barrow Island, George, Albert and William were all fishermen.

George Brown was a rum character and also a kind-hearted individual. I only met him once. This was around 1959 at the time he was teaching my father how to knit fishing nets (George could have knitted nets in his sleep!). For our nets, dad sourced the string (twine) from the Gourock Rope Company's outlet at Fleetwood. I recall going there twice, once by rail and later by road. After making our purchase the day would be spent looking around Wyre Dock and the resident fishing fleet. It would then conclude with a fish supper, usually hake and chips.

The Gourock Rope Company started in Gourock, Scotland in 1736. It incorporated as a limited company in 1903. The company became a world leader manufacturing ropes and sails for schooners. Over the years, and after becoming an international concern, other products, such as netting, twine and hardware were made. In 1970 the concern was acquired by British Ropes Limited.

George Brown's second home at the time was, arguably, the bar of the Royal Hotel, Barrow Island (he would knit and repair nets for beer money). George's wife, Kate, had worked in the Dockers' Canteen. This was accessed by crossing the railway line at the end of St Andrew's Street, Barrow Island.

The Brown's boat, Bluebell (BW10), had been in the family a long time. In 1935 it would be involved in tragedy. William (Billy) one of the brothers, had taken Bluebell fishing for mackerel on the evening of 30th July, 1935. He was never seen alive again. Having no luck spinning Billy decided to start trawling for fluke, in an area off the south end of Walney known as Kendal Hill. This was witnessed by a boat called Thora, also fishing, and which was in the vicinity about half a mile distant. The last Hugh Molyneux, the Thora's skipper, saw of Bluebell was when Billy reefed his sail – which indicated that he was about to haul in the net. It must have been at this point that Billy, a non-swimmer, went over the side becoming entangled in the trawl.

George Brown searched the tide every night for a month hoping to find his brother.

Billy's body was eventually washed up on the west shore of Walney Island. George was called to identify his brother's emaciated body. Billy was just 37-years old! Up to this time George had been a non-drinker. He never recovered from the ordeal of losing his brother, or his resulting taste for alcohol. Conducting the inquest, the Deputy Coroner, Mr J. Poole, issued a verdict of 'Accidental drowning while fishing off Walney'.

In conversation with George's daughter, Margaret Burrow, she told me:

In 1947 George was admitted to a TB Hospital in Oswestry, leaving Kate to look after six children and a 4-day old baby. George was in the hospital for two years. He spent his time there knitting fishing nets. After leaving Oswestry George was unable to hold a physical job of work for several years. He did, however, put his trawl nets to good use. He would take fish back to the flat on Barrow Island. These were then put onto wire (strings of fish). Margaret and her siblings were then sent out to distribute the fish among neighbours. The Brown children detested the fishy smell that pervaded their home but more importantly, they thought the practice of skewering them onto wires was cruel (Margaret, to this day has not eaten fish!).

It is only now, she went on to say, does she realise how astute her father was in putting good food on people's tables at a time when the war had savaged the Country's finances.

Two years later George went back into the shipyard as a platers' helper. He died in 1979, five years after his beloved Kate.

Albert Theodore (Tuddy) Urry was another personality I was introduced to in the late 1950s. As well as down the beach, he was also a well-known and popular Walney character. *Tuddy,* along with Osmand Wood, was a founder member of Walney's Nautical Club. He lived on King Alfred Street, Walney with his wife Agnes and daughter, Janice. *Tuddy* worked in the shipyard as a fitter and turner. He had two boats, first the *Pioneer* and later the *Flying Fish.* I have no recollection of either. He would also crew on the *June* with the Parkinson brothers and they regularly sailed to Glasson Dock and the Isle of Man. My source told me that they would often cruise down the Channel to Piel Island and spend the day in the Ship Inn. Janice, who was a musician, would play such as sea shanties and popular tunes on the bar piano.

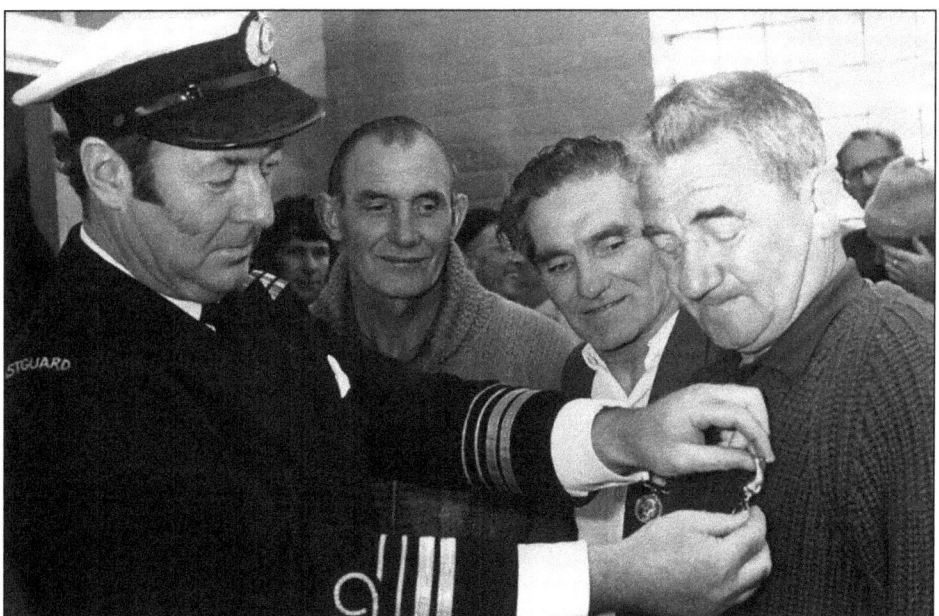

Tuddy Urry (right) receiving his long-service medal from a coastguard official. Of those known are: second from left Bill Bartlett; Bert Booth (*Largo*); Dougie Moore; Simmy Sadler.

*The **Pioneer** at Chapel Bed c. 1959. Both images courtesy of Janice Urry.*

Mr Urry would sometimes be down the beach in his official capacity as Coastguard Officer. I remember him turning up with Frank Stutchberry in the Coastguard van. *Tuddy* also did a regular shift in the Coastguard Station on the Island's west coast. The CG lookout tower was accessed from Mill Lane, being sited at the end of Fort Road.

Other old-timers known but only on a casual basis, were: Jack Frost; Tommy Newton; Frank Posnett; Ben Revell; George (old-man) Sloan and Jack Tordoff. The likes of Jack Frost and Ben Revell would go 'down the beach' to simply potter. They had boats beached in front of their sheds (which in my time down there never went out), and which they worked on, drank tea, chatted and smoked. They were obviously content in doing just this.

4

The Boats

Believe me there is nothing – absolute nothing – half so much worth doing as simply messing about in boats.

During the period under review there were three main classes of boat on Ferry Beach. These were the yachts, the Morecambe Bay prawners and the converted ship's lifeboats. In addition to a variety of punts and dinghies, there was also the individualistic vessels. Names like *Acco* (Dr Taylor); *Gladys; Briar;* Ronny Atha's *Crusader;* George Harper's *Tuskar* and Osmand Wood's *Williwaw* spring immediately to mind.

The Merchant Shipping Act of 1894 required all British sea fishing boats, irrespective of size, to be registered (lettered and numbered).

The many sailing boats, apart from *White Rose, Breeze* and the *Dairy Maid*, previously mentioned, are beyond the scope of this book.

PRAWNERS

Although some prawners were built at Overton and also Fleetwood, the main builder in the area was Crossfields of Arnside, Lancashire. This was in the period - 1850 to 1930. Prawners were a very sturdy yet graceful class of boat, being instantly recognisable by their low, overhung counters. Many were subsequently converted to yachts and pleasure craft.

Crossfields were builders of yachts, prawners (also known as Lancashire Nobbies) and sailing dinghies. John Crossfield, a ships carpenter, arrived in Arnside in 1818 and established a joinery business. His younger son Francis developed the boat building side of the business in 1838. By 1880 the business was being run by John's sons – William, Francis, John and George and trading as Crossfield Brothers. They advertised themselves as 'Joiners, Undertakers, Builders; Yacht and Boat Builders'. Their yard (Top Yard), was located on Church Hill. At a later date another yard, the Beach Walk Yard, was opened by eldest son William. This continued up to the 1940s by which time the demand for their output had declined. When Frederick, the last of the Crossfields retired, the Beach Walk Yard became the 'Crossfield Successors'. Run firstly by a John Gill until 1966, and then by a John Deurden until 1983, the yard finally closed its doors in 1985.

The Crossfield signature product was without doubt the Morecambe Bay Prawner. These were fast, gaff rigged boats designed to sail and work the shallow waters of the North West Coast. Their distinctive features are the elliptical stern, central cockpit with a large deck area and low freeboard for working the nets. The size of boat produced at Arnside ranged from 22-foot to 40-feet in length being supplied to ports from North Wales to southern Scotland.

Upon receiving an order to build they would first make a scale model for owner approval. It would then take four men 6-weeks to build a 32-footer. Construction was usually larch planking on oak frames.

(With acknowledgements to and paraphrased from an article in the Westmorland Gazette, Dec 2018).

Perhaps the oldest, and maybe the fastest, prawner on Ferry Beach was Bill Dickinson's *Maggie* (BW125). She was a 28-footer (always painted white) and by the late 1950s was letting in water. Despite her condition, *Dicko* kept her busy (trawling) and powered by a Kelvin petrol/paraffin marine engine, her sleek hull form meant she was ultra-fast. Sometime after 1963 the *Maggie* left Ferry Beach for Maryport, Cumberland.

(Bill Dickinson occupied the hut next-door to ours on the Ferry pitching).

Banshee is a 22-footer weighing in at 1¼ tons. Her sister ships on Ferry Beach were *Thistle* and *Teal*. Banshee is unusual for a prawner, being a double-ender (she was most probably a shrimp boat). Built at Lancaster in 1866, she was originally used by the Charnley family as a pilot cutter. The *West Cumberland Advertiser* of 15 December, 1987 noted:

Barrow's Maritime (Dock) Museum is yet to be built but already there is a growing collection of items bought and donated which will show off the area's boating and shipping past. The latest acquisition is a 22-foot prawner, Banshee. She has been bought by the museum with the help of a grant from the Science Museum. Mr David Hughes, curator of the Furness Museum, said: "We are very grateful to the Science Museum for the grant which enabled us to buy the Banshee and also to VSEL, who have kindly agreed to store her for us until she can be brought to the Maritime Museum. There is a news cutting from 1866 which reports a boat being overset in a squall. Two members of the Charnley family survived but a young boy – also a Charnley –

Banshee high and dry at Barrow's Dock Museum, 2022.
S. Henderson collection.

Empress, minus her mast and standing rigging, on Ferry Beach in 1965. *Trawlerpictures.net (Norman)*

was missing presumed dead. Banshee was later found waterlogged a few miles from where she overturned. (Barrow's Dock Museum was opened in 1994).

In conversation with Trevor Swindells, last owner of *Banshee* (1980s), Trevor stated that she is not a prawner but actually a 'Wyre-Whammel' or salmon boat. During the 1980s she was powered by a Stuart Turner petrol engine. He also claimed that she was the last sail-boat pilot cutter of the district.

George Sloan's *Empress* (BW115) was possibly the best maintained fishing boat on the beach during my recall. She was a 34-footer[***], built in 1928 by Crossfields. She was always painted battleship grey with a red belting and was of a deeper draught than the typical

---

[***] *Empress* was registered as being a 30-footer. Was this 'mistake' so that she could fish inshore?

prawner. Her defining feature was the truncated counter (transom). She seemed unique in this regard. *Empress* was powered by a Lister marine diesel engine which also provided power to her winch. Owner, George Sloan Jr. was a strict skipper who took his job (trawling) very seriously. Judd, as he was called, accepted nothing short of one hundred percent commitment and loyalty from his crew – Skev Evans and Mike Gardner.

The *Empress* went to the Isle of Man regularly, usually during Vickers's holiday fortnight. She left Ferry Beach in the late 1960s for Workington.

(The prawner *Empress* was Sloan's second boat with this name. His earlier Empress was a 28-foot converted lifeboat [BW14], registered in 1949).

The *Cricket* (BW72) was another Crossfield's boat. She came to Barrow as an open boat, half-decked (no cabin or dodger). A 28 footer, always painted blue, and always appeared to be on her mooring. This was south of *Falcon's* mooring which was the northern-most and just west of the Steps on the Barrow side. The line-up as I recall was *Falcon; Cricket; Star of Hope; White Rose* and then the *Sea King,* all deep-water moorings.

Cricket's owner was Charles Edward (Eddie) Stutchberry of Clive Street, Hindpool. Eddie and his brother, Frank, had owned boats on Ferry Beach since the end of the war.

Ruby underway on Walney Channel. She had been in the Quayle family for 80 years. *Photo, Walney Webs*

Ruby is a 28-foot prawner, owned for many years by shipwright Dennis Quayle, of Walney Island. Dennis also owned the *Tern* (BW100) at one time. *Ruby* was built in 1890 at the yard of J. Gibson and Son, Fleetwood. Prawners built at Fleetwood were known as half-deckers, they also tended to be deeper draughted than those from Arnside. Ruby's hull was close-seamed larch on oak frames and was one of four built as sailing ferries (Fleetwood to Knott End). Ruby was brought to Barrow in 1917 for the purpose of fishing, being registered as BW7. During my recall she was either at Ferry Beach or moored south of the Bridge on Chapel Bed. Despite her name, she was always painted green.

In more recent times *Ruby* is in the capable hands of Neil Morrison.

CONVERTED LIFEBOATS

During the Second World War boating on Walney Channel was subject to very strict government control. Access to Ferry Beach was even restricted, with a policeman always on duty. When hostilities eventually ceased, Ferry Beach became a place of interest to would-be mariners who must have felt the call of the sea! Young men, perhaps recently demobbed, decided to venture into boating. The catalyst for this, which enabled working-class folk with limited means, was Ward's ship-breakers who operated at the northern-end of Devonshire Dock. Wards, depending on what they were breaking, was a veritable *Aladdin's Cave* for anyone building or converting small craft. Ship's lifeboats could be purchased for the price of £1 per linear foot, as well as masts, booms, spars and oars. There was an

A Lifeboat conversion ongoing (even before completion she seems to be observing flag etiquette!). *Andrew Clark collection.*

assortment of ship's fittings such as SOLAS equipment (life-jackets, life belts etc.), punkah louvres, handrails, deck fittings like cleats, shackles and turnbuckles, flags and pennants. The man in charge of this 'chandlery' was Jack Houldsworth (Big Jack) who lived on Anson Street, Hindpool. A person's priority regarding the purchase of certain items and even the price they paid was totally dependent upon their standing with Big Jack!

It was from Wards, in 1952, that my father and his three partners bought the *Falcon*. They were fortunate in that the vessel came with some preliminary outfitting and at the time of purchase was deployed by Wards as a runabout in Devonshire Dock. The boat came already engined. It had a Morris Navigator marine petrol engine which propelled it along at a good 5 – 6 knots. The first modification undertaken was converting the engine to the more economical paraffin. This involved the fitting of a 'hot-box'. Next was the finishing-off of the topsides (superstructure) by building a wheelhouse (dodger). A suit of sails (red canvas) was obtained. This comprised a foresail (jib) and a gaff mainsail. The mainsail had the boat's registration number, BW 49, emblazoned in white lettering. Jamming cleats were fitted to the cockpit coaming, port and starboard, for controlling the jib sheets. The main sheet horse was fixed atop the wheelhouse. (Because of their shape below the waterline, lifeboats could not sail to windward [tack], so you tended to motor sail. They could, however, run before the wind, thereby still affording the thrill of sailing).

For several years my mother would not allow me to go out on fishing trips, she could not trust dad to keep his eye on me. My father was a very self-assured individual. Nothing seemed to faze him, so getting lost at sea with him, or anywhere for that matter, would not have been a problem.

Outings on the *Falcon* were either fishing trips or pleasure excursions to Piel Island. The latter invariably involved my mother and sisters, Joan and Margery. On occasion we would go out to Morecambe Flats and do some kebbing. The Flats were reached by steaming for 20-minutes from Seldom Seen towards Blackpool Tower and then dropping anchor. The water in this area was crystal-clear and you could sometimes see the fish taking your bait.

During the summer months Piel would be crowded with day-trippers who had crossed from Roa on the Moore's ferry boat. On one occasion, during 1958, while we were enjoying some time on Piel, I recall that TV personality Hughie Green, along with his entourage, had sailed from the Isle of Man in his motor yacht *Rake's Retreat*. They commandeered the bar of the *Ship Inn*.

A fishing trip usually involved setting off with a crew of four, about three hours after high water and with the punt in tow - which carried the trammel net. Upon reaching Piel, the punt, with its crew of two and British Seagull outboard motor, headed for either Bass Pool or Ragman Light (Foulney Island) where the 100-yard net would be shot. The 'big boat' continued up towards Ulverston Channel to a corner of Morecambe Bay referred to as Back of the Lights, where it would start trawling. On the return trip the punt, with its catch, would be taken back in tow for the journey home. During the return trip the catch would be sorted. A typical trawl, which lasted around thirty minutes, could yield, apart from seaweed and starfish, about two stones of good fish. These would be mainly plaice fluke, flounders and sangsters. There may also have been the odd lemon sole, an eel or two and some crabs. With the catch graded and the undersized fish thrown back, my father would start making up strings of fish (using wire). During the period discussed, a string of fish (comprising 5 or 6 fish) was sold for half-a-dollar or 2 shillings and sixpence [half a crown] in old money.

Occasionally, Bert Jackson, my father's boss at the Steelworks, who was on the crew of *Herbert Leigh*, would join us on fishing trips. On one particular trip Mr Jackson told us of a rescue he was involved with concerning a member of his family and the pilot boat – Argus. A junior engineer on the boat was fatally injured while effecting a repair.

Trinity House Pilot Vessel *MV Argus* pictured off Roa Island. She was a single-screw 40-footer (wooden hull), with a 12 foot beam and drawing 4.8 ft. Argus was powered by a 44 bhp Kelvin diesel. She was built in 1935 by James N. Miller & Sons at their St Monance Yard, Scotland. (Argus was usually moored in the Channel, just off the Harbour Yard).

The *N. W. Evening Mail* of 17 December, 1957 reported:

> *John Hughes of Roa Island, a boatman with the Trinity House Pilots at Barrow, today sustained fatal injuries while working below decks aboard the Argus. Hughes, who was in his early 20s, was attempting to clear a choked bilge pump and was caught by the propeller shaft. He sustained a broken arm and a broken jaw and suffered severe shock. He died on the way to North Lonsdale Hospital.*
>
> *The Argus had put out that morning to take Mr Roland Moore, a pilot and coxswain of Barrow lifeboat, to a tanker bound for*

Heysham. The pilot boat was then to take a Mr Ralph Hoffman, another pilot, off the Cora, bound for Glasgow.

While proceeding to the Cora, Jackson Charnley and Hughes, the two boatmen of Argus, noticed the bilge pump appeared to be choked. Hughes, the second mechanic aboard the Barrow lifeboat, went below to deal with the trouble. His companion heard a thump and the boat's engine stopped.

Going below, Mr Charnley found Hughes apparently caught by the propeller shaft badly hurt and in a confined space. Charnley tried to call Seaforth radio on the boat's radio telephone and then took a chance and called the Barrow lifeboat. The call was intercepted by Mr Frank Moore, mechanic on the lifeboat, who summoned the crew.

The Lifeboat came up with Argus off the South End of Walney where the pilot boat had drifted aground whilst Mr Charnley was attempting to give aid to Hughes.

Members of Barrow lifeboat went by punt to the grounded Argus and managed to free Hughes. They waded ashore carrying Hughes on a stretcher to an awaiting ambulance.

Onboard the lifeboat was Hughes' father, Mr Jim Hughes, a member of Barrow Fire Brigade and also a lifeboatman, also Mr Bert Jackson, John Hughe's brother-in-law. (Extract).

Barracuda (BW177): a 29-footer; clinker-built; registered in 1963. Skippered by Bill Bowron. Joint owners were: Robert Nelson; William Bowron and George Brown Jr.

Crack 'o Noon (BW211): a 28-footer owned by John Alexander (Alec) McAloone of Cameron Street, Barrow Island.

Falcon (BW49): a 28-footer; 9.5ft beam; clinker built. Joint owners: N. Adams; M. Gifford; Major Bromley and Stan Henderson. Registered skipper: S. Henderson.

In 1964 Falcon was sold to a Fred Rennie of Sloop Street, Barrow Island. (There had been an earlier *Falcon* on Ferry Beach (BW91), a 26-footer of which I have no recollection. It was owned by a Stan Lauder of Strathmore Avenue, Walney. Registered in 1945).

Charlie Barnard's *Yonder* (BW87). Apart from being a foot wider in the beam, *Falcon* was almost identical. Unfortunately no photos of *Falcon* survive. *Courtesy of Mavis Barnard.*

Greylag (BW74): 26-footer; clinker-built; owned by Eddie Stutchberry. Registered in 1957. No further information available.

June: 30-foot, double-diagonal, pleasure craft. Diesel powered. Owners were the Parkinson brothers, Arthur (ex RN) and Ken. June made regular trips to Fleetwood, Glasson Dock and the Isle of Man.

Largo (BW166): 30-foot, double diagonal; cabin cruiser. Diesel powered. Registered in 1962. Owner/skipper Herbert (Bert) Booth of Verdun Avenue Walney. Eddie Booth, crewman. *Largo* was a regular visitor to the Isle of Man, usually during Vickers holiday fortnight.

Merry Kettle: 28-footer; clinker-built; pleasure boat. Owners; Kitchen brothers. Moored in the Ferry Hole which was a sought-after deep-water mooring. The *'Kettle'* was used mainly for booze cruises. This would be where, for example, after the Wheatsheaf had kicked-out on a Sunday afternoon in summer. Jimmy Kitchen would take a party down to the Ship on Piel to continue drinking. On occasion they would cross the Bay to Fleetwood. The *Kettle* later passed to Frank Posnett of Goldsmith Street, Hindpool, who registered her, in 1959 for trawling, as BW19.

Mischief: 24-foot (BW 180), clinker-built; registered in 1962. Owner/skipper: Dougie Ayres. The vessel changed hands several times over the years.

Rose: 26-foot, carvel-built ex lifeboat outfitted as a cabin cruiser. Owner/skipper: Frank Stutchberry (also an auxiliary Coast Guard).

Rover: 26-foot (BW 136), clinker-built; owner/skipper: Jack Davies.

Sea King: 28-foot (BW 84), clinker-built; registered in 1957. Owners: Bud and John Evans. *Sea King* was the only boat in my recall to exit Walney Channel to the north and trawl the Duddon Channel.

Star of Hope: a 27-footer (BW45), clinker-built; powered by a Kelvin petrol/paraffin engine. Owner/skipper: Cecil Nicholas. The boat benefitted from having its propeller housed in a tunnel. This was achieved by Ces undertaking a large modification to the hull planking immediately forward of the sternpost. (When out in choppy seas, a lifeboat's propeller would often come out of the water leading to loss of headway and causing the engine to race. Having the propeller in a tunnel eliminated this).

Example of a propeller housed in a tunnel (*RNLB Herbert Leigh*). *S. Henderson collection.*

Oddjob and *Star of Hope* moored in the Channel c. 1984. *Courtesy of Brian Moxham.*

Tony (BW193): was a 28-footer, clinker-built and powered by a Morris car engine converted to TVO. Registered in 1952. Owner/skipper: Bill Thompson. Bill sold the *Tony* in 1958/59 when he joined *Falcon's* crew.

Tuskar (BW105): was a sort of hybrid but, because she was originally a ship's lifeboat, I have included her in this section of the book. She belonged to George Aukland Harper, a time-served joiner.

Tuskar was a 28-footer, clinker built double-ender. George put his woodworking skills to work and gave her a transom stern and also a crafted hard wood, polished, wheelhouse. He registered her for fishing in 1957.

Tuskar **at her mooring in the Channel c. 1984.** *Courtesy of Brian Moxham.*

THE INDIVIDUAL BOATS

Briar (BW175): appeared on Ferry Beach early in 1960 when she was beached next to our boat. Her owner/skipper Les *Moff* Gardner of Annan Street, Barrow Island, was using Bill Dickinson's boat store while he undertook some work on her engine. Briar was powered by a 4-cylinder Gardner marine diesel. This engine also powered the trawl winch *via* a mechanical drive mechanism.

I immediately struck-up a friendship with Les, he was an affable lad, about 26-years old. *Moff* allowed me to look around his new boat – I think he sensed my keenness!

Briar was a seiner/trawler typical of the class that fished out of Whitehaven at the time (flush-deckers). I put her at, about, 32-feet long with a 4-foot draught. Although referred to in archives as a small fishing boat, the local authorities, upon registration, insisted she was too big to fish inshore!

Briar comprised two transverse bulkheads effectively dividing her into three compartments. Aftermost was the engine room. Forward of this was the fish hold and then the accommodation. Access to each compartment was *via* a hatch in the upper deck.

What I found surprising about her was just how basic she was! Just a big engine and a trawl winch sat in a, very sound, hull. There was absolutely no equipment, no semblance of a galley, no interior lighting nor instruments of any kind. The wheelhouse was of just sufficient size to accommodate the helmsman and there were no engine controls at this position!

One thing that my father had always stressed were these two rules: 1. Never take a boat out fishing unaccompanied and, 2. Never take out a boat under the influence of alcohol. Les Gardner, as with Billy Brown, fell foul of rule 1.

Briar on Ferry Beach, early 1960s; Photo *Trawlerpictures.net (Norman)*

Moff would take the *Briar* fishing on his own. During the summer of 1960 it nearly cost him his life!

The Log of Rescues by RNLB *Herbert Leigh* for 25 June, 1960, recorded the following:

> *Briar was trawling approximately 2-miles west of Lightning Knoll (sea state moderate, force 3). A tanker in the vicinity (Kellia) had radioed Formby Coastguard, at 3.30pm, that a 'yacht' alongside, with a one-man crew, where it appeared the mast had fallen and broken the man's arm. The man was in a semi-conscious state and that a doctor was required immediately. The Herbert Leigh reached the scene at 4.45pm and found the fishing boat*

Briar alongside the Kellia. The master/owner was aboard his vessel with a compound fracture of the upper right arm and he had lost a lot of blood. He was treated by the emergency medic and then transferred to the lifeboat. Herbert Leigh then took the Briar in tow.

Statement by Mr R. Moore, Hon Sec of the Lifeboat Service noted: *The Briar was fishing near to the Kellia and the owner was hauling in his net by winch when his arm was caught and taken around the winch drum. The second mate of the tanker heard him scream and swarmed down a rope over the stern as the Briar drifted past. The vessel's mast was down in the stowed position and it was presumed that it had fallen and broken his arm.*

RNLB *Herbet Leigh* underway. Frank Moore is at the rail (amidships, peaked cap), Peter Charnley is to Frank's left, c. 1960. *Courtesy of the Dock Museum (BAWMS 09992.03)).*

The lifeboat's crew on the day were: R. Moore, Cox; N. Charnley, 2nd Cox; J. Vaughan; B. Jackson; T. Barber; F. Moore, Mechanic and R.O. Charnley, Assistant Mechanic.

I remember seeing *Moff* about one month after his accident. He showed me his *mangled* arm and I was shocked. His injuries were horrific! It was a miracle that he didn't lose his arm completely.

It is recorded in the Register of Fishing Boats that *Briar* was destroyed by fire in 1968. (In 1967 Les Gardner bought a 19-footer called *Osprey*).

Gladys, BW4, originally PL61, was registered at Barrow in July, 1939. She had been beached for the full time span covered by this book. During this period I never saw anyone, owners or otherwise, giving her any attention. My father told me that she had left the Isle of Man for Barrow in 1936.

Gladys was a Manx Nobby of 12-tons, built in 1901-02 at Peel, Isle of Man, by Neakle & Watterson as a fishing (Herring) smack.

Gladys on Ferry Beach in October, 1975.
Photo D.J. Hughes courtesy of Manx National Heritage.

She was 41-feet in length, 12-feet six inches beam and with a draught of 6-feet. Her location on Ferry Beach was mid-way between the Clubhouse and the Ferry ticket office. Her style, shape and vintage brought her many admirers. She had three registered owners: John William Harper of Buller Street, Walney. Herbert Heavyside of Andover Street, Barrow Island. and a John James ? of Beech Street, Barrow.****

The Crusader had been on Ferry Beach prior to my recall. I did not know her owner personally (Ronny Atha). Although deployed, mainly, for pleasure trips to Piel, she had been registered for fishing, as BW178, in 1947. She was also regularly used on the launch timber retrieval runs, receiving a fee from Vickers Armstrong for this service.

Crusader on her mooring. *Courtesy of Brian Moxham.*

**** Gladys left Ferry Beach in 1975. She has been refurbished and now sails around the Cornish coast.

Crusader beached at North Scale, Walney Island in Dec '22.

The Williwaw was a 28-footer, double-diagonal construction, and built at Barrow in 1938. I do not know what class of vessel she was. She was owned by local businessman Ozzie Wood of Chairman's Walk, Walney. (No further details available).

Note: Many of the foregoing had changed hands several times over the years. The owners/skippers listed are of my main recall and probably the original keepers. The *Williwaw*, for instance, was registered by Osmand Wood but my source told me that in 1967, she passed to an Eric Picton.

NB: Referring to a boat as being a 28-footer was Ferry Beach-Speak meaning LOA: 28ft.

Afterword

Red sails in the sunset, way out on the sea...

Walney Channel, especially Ferry Beach, was an oyster very rich in pearls!

The Channel during the fifties and early sixties was a busy thoroughfare. Ships laden with cargoes of iron ore; wood pulp; timber; grain and coal were regularly seen - all keeping the Trinity House Pilots active.

Converted ship's lifeboats were a once familiar site on Walney Channel. In fact they could be seen on any UK waterway. They displayed the imagination and creativity of the converter, giving a characterful motor boat; fishing smack or 'yacht'. In many instances their owners were amateurs in the field of boat building – but they had a passion. I believe it was this passion that communicated itself to me as an impressionable youngster. Post millennium, they have become, sadly, very rare but as they form part of our maritime history they are worth preserving. This book is an attempt to preserve some of that history.

Since my account of times spent on Ferry Beach over sixty years ago, things have taken a quantum leap forward. During the period discussed there were no such things as folding propellers, automatic helmsmen, ship-to-shore communications or satellite navigation. You sailed to the Isle of Man with just a compass, a chart and your ability in seamanship. During the 1950s things like Terylene sails and anti-fouling paint were just beginning to appear. But still, you needed the money to avail yourself of those items. When our boat was laid-up for her annual paint job we relied on a mate getting a tin of red lead or some white paint for us, from the shipyard! (If you had the contacts, you could even get a stern-tube made there). Everything in those far-off days seemed to be based on beg, borrow or steal (or barter)!

Ferry Beach survives through the good offices of Barrow Sailing Club who have made many improvements since the 1960s. There are now virtually no lifeboat conversions to be seen and no boats beached in front of the boat stores, as before. They, along with their owners, have all decayed. The enthusiasm for Ferry Beach, displayed by the group of happy-go-lucky mariners - once evident during my time there - has now gone.

Sources

Literary quotes:

Frontispiece: *Sea-Fever*; John Masefield.

Origins: *Ferry Me Across the Water*; Christina Rossetti.

Barrow Sailing Club: *The West Wind*; John Masefield.

Down the Beach: *Over My Toes. . .*; Michael Rosen.

The Boats: *Believe Me There is Nothing. . .* Kenneth Grahame.

Afterword: *Red sails in the sunset. . .* J. Kennedy/ J. Grosz.

Appendix: *The Walrus and the Carpenter. . .* Lewis Carroll

Local Records:

Register of Fishing Boats: Cumbria Archives & Local Study Centre (Barrow).

Log of Rescues by RNLB Herbert Leigh (*Minute Book*): Ibid.

Maternal Family History. Leasil Burrow (Brown).

Charles Turner (1899-1960). A Memoir.

Publications Consulted:

Graces Industrial Guides, online.

Alan Lockett, '*Morecambe Bay*' (1973)

Alan Lockett, *North-western Ships and Seamen* (1982)

North West Evening Mail, Tuesday, 17 December, 1957.

West Cumberland Advertiser, December 1987.

Westmorland Gazette, December, 2018.

Tony Diamond, *Shipwreck and Boating Accidents of Barrow and District.* (1982)

Websites:

Nobbyownersassociation.co.uk/members-boats

Trawlerpictures.net

rich@exlifeboat.co.uk

Walney Webs

Personal communications:

Margaret Burrow (née Brown) MBE; Evadne Evans; Norman Pascoe; Trevor Swindells; Paul Turner and Janice Urry.

Appendix

The time has come the Walrus said ...

PRIME MOVERS

During the 1950s, lifeboat conversions were mainly powered by car engines that had been sourced from local scrapyards. This was because the average working man, usually with a young family to support, did not have the means to buy a proper marine engine – not even a second hand one! These car engines would be adapted to run on the cheaper paraffin or tractor vapourising oil (TVO) as it was called. TVO has a lower octane rating than petrol and so the engines still needed to be started on petrol. Upon reaching normal running temperature you could switch over to paraffin. In those days we used to purchase our TVO, by the gallon, from Unsworth's Dominion Street Garage on Walney. From around 1960, a West Cumberland Farmers tanker would visit Ferry Beach regularly and we would then buy it in lots of 40-gallons. Also around 1960, second-hand Kelvin marine engines, again petrol/paraffin with magneto ignition, made an appearance. Some boats also had marine diesels fitted. The large majority of these engines had to be hand-cranked. It would be a while before electric starting appeared.

Building the *Daisy* 1. The deadwood and keel are clearly visible. Note the white lead around the keel bolts. C.1960. *Andrew Clark Collection.*

Building the *Daisy* 2. Ces Nicholas checking-out frames for the stringers. C.1960. *Andrew Clark Collection.*

Building the *Daisy* 3. The roll-out. C.1962. *Andrew Clark Collection.*

Building the *Daisy* 4. The finished product. C.1962. *Andrew Clark Collection.*

TRINITY HOUSE PILOTAGE – a brief synopsis

Trinity House is a charity dedicated to safeguarding shipping and seafarers with also a statutory duty as a General Lighthouse Authority, for the benefit of all mariners.

Incorporated by Royal Charter (Henry VIII) in 1514. Today it is the UK's largest-endowed maritime charity.

In the early days local fishermen, because of their knowledge of local waters, doubled as pilots. The Charnley family, who are mentioned in this book and also Roland Moore, Coxswain of the Barrow Lifeboat, acted as pilots for the Barrow and Fleetwood Approaches.

Trinity House Pilots also worked closely with HM Coastguard. From my days on Ferry Beach I recall meeting and speaking to Theodore Urry, a Coastguard officer. Mr Urry was a regular down the beach, he had involvement with the Pilots.

For further reading about Trinity House, see *Light Upon The Waters*, by R. Woodman and A. Adams.

Miscellaneous boats adjacent to the Clubhouse, 1980s. *Andrew Clark Collection.*

Boats in front of the (old) boat stores, 1980s. The N.W. Shop of Vickers dominates the background. 1980s.

FERRY BEACH – TIDE MOVEMENT

Walney Channel south of the Bridge is buoyed and was dredged regularly. The buoys extend for about 6-miles out to Lightning Knoll, which was the first, or last encountered, depending upon your heading. There are two tides per day in Walney Channel with extreme ranges of depth. These can be 33-feet (10m) Spring Tides and 22-feet (6.7m) Neap Tides.

Due to the fact that the incoming tide floods from both north and south of the Island, the two torrents coalesce at a location called 'The Meetings', causing periods of slack water to occur either side of high water. The Meetings are an area of shallows about three-quarters of a mile north of the Bridge, the area is mainly dry until, about 2-hours before HW.

North of the Bridge and for Ferry Beach the current, on the flood, runs at about 2-knots until 40-minutes before high water. Shortly after high water there is another brief period of slack and then the tide turns and runs south until low water.

Local knowledge and experience are needed when navigating the Channel to the north.

As the old proverb says: *'Time and tide wait for no man'*.

NAUTICAL STUDIES

During the period covered by this book, Holker County Secondary School had an open lifeboat moored on the Walney side of the Channel. This was used by those pupils taking Nautical Studies. It is recalled that every Wednesday in summer, weather permitting, a group of lads from the school, under the tutelage of teacher, Ernie Diamond, would row the vessel around the Channel at 'slack water'. Mr Diamond lived at either Roa or Rampside and was a crew member of the *RNLB Herbert Leigh*.

Example of a converted ship's lifeboat.

SHIPS' LIFEBOATS

In the days of volume shipbuilding in this country some of the larger yards constructed their own lifeboats. Two of the main boat-builders specialising in wooden lifeboat construction, were Samuel White at their Falcon Works, Cowes, on the Isle-of-Wight and J. Pounder & Co of Throston Bridge, Hartlepool.

The standard construction was clinker (lapstrake), for boats 28-feet long and below. Those over 28-feet in length tended to be either carvel planked (Larch) or double-diagonal.

During the first 30-years of the twentieth century, wooden lifeboats were mass-produced by Pounders to specifications issued by the Board of Trade. It is interesting to ponder the fact that lifeboats were made in the hope that they would never be used. The irony is that the skilled boat builders at Pounders Boat Yard would have had no way of knowing that, after twenty or so years, some of the fruits of their labour would bring joy and pleasure to so many!

The interior of Pounder's workshop, Hartlepool. *1920s.*

Lifeboats loaded onto railway flat-beds for onward transmission to a shipyard customer. 1920s.
Images courtesy of Callum and Ritchie.

Map of the Irish Sea showing the location of the Briar on 26 June, 1960.

The Author

Stan Henderson is a Cumbrian senior citizen. He was born, reared and schooled in Hindpool, Barrow-in-Furness. His ancestors came to the district in 1876 to work in the local iron works.

Stan served an apprenticeship at Barrow Shipyard, working for 25-years as a ship draughtsman. He later moved into Quality Assurance. Since reaching retirement age he has researched the local iron and steel industry and has documented his research in previous publications and, as with this work, the books are sold in support of the emergency services.

Also by the author ...

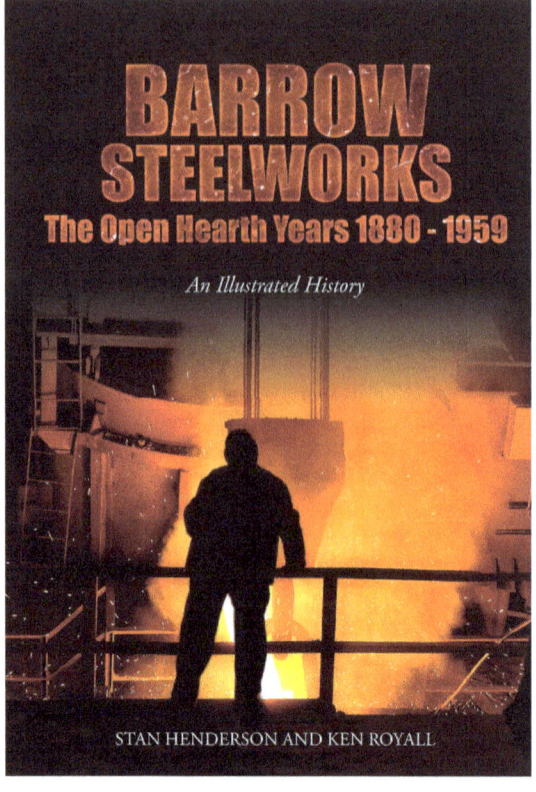

During the second half of the nineteenth century, Barrow-in-Furness became a pioneer in iron and steel production. It went on to grow astronomically – owning collieries in three counties and ore mines in two – and became the largest integrated steelworks in north Lancashire and Cumberland and, at one time, the largest steelworks in the world. Its success was due, in part, to having the prestige of three dukes as directors, as well as to being only 2 miles away from one of the largest and richest iron ore mines in the country.

The 1880s were a decade of change for Barrow works with some of the main players departing the scene. The arrival of the basic method of steelmaking, took away the lucrative position held by the directors and shareholders who had drained the coffers leaving virtually nothing for re-investment. After the Great War the company was limping along. The evacuation of Dunkirk at the start of WWII together with the blocking of special steels produced a demand for the kind of steel the making of which Barrow was a past master. Under United Steel's banner Barrow would see security of employment.

Paperback: 160 pages
Publisher: The History Press;
Language: English
ISBN-13: 978-0750963787

Paperback: 98 pages
Publisher: Stanley Henderson
Language: English
ISBN-13: 978-0995619050

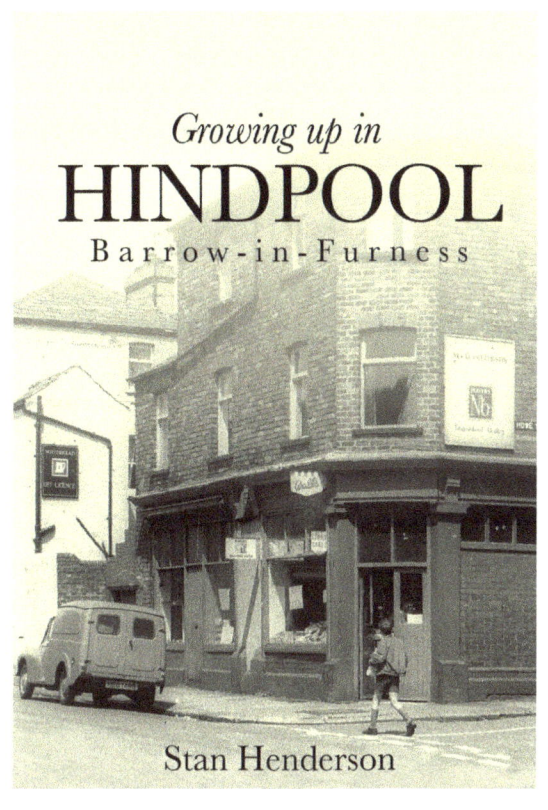
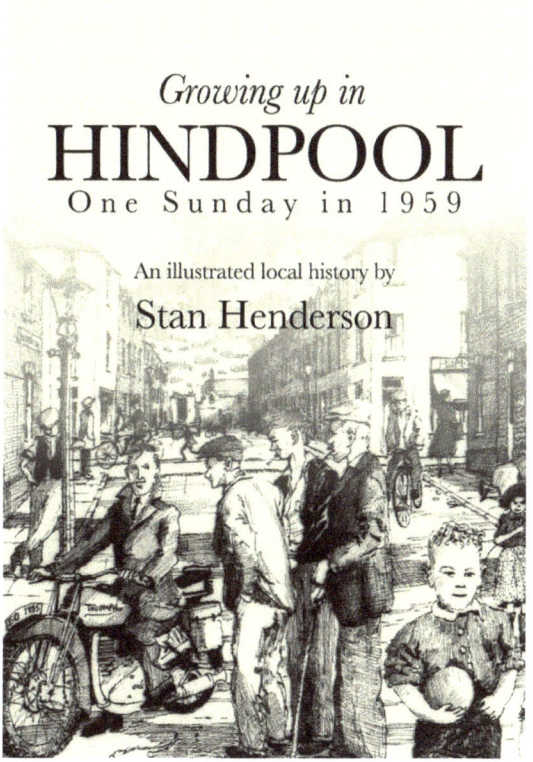

The history of Hindpool has been likened to a patchwork quilt, with each fragment, or patch, different in time, size, shape and colour. In his book the author has woven his quilt with the thread of family history and personal experience. The story starts with the arrival in Barrow of the writer's ancestors, immigrants from Shropshire, who had come to work on the blast furnaces of the local, monster, Ironworks. These works would later hold an unexplained fascination for the author, who, in this book takes the reader on a conducted tour around the historic works.

In this follow-up to Growing Up in Hindpool, the author completes his patchwork quilt with respect to the industries, institutions and businesses to which he has been directly or indirectly involved. The reader is taken on a walk out of the district and, via Lower Cocken, into Ormsgill, then back into Hindpool. During this walk, which 60-years ago, was undertaken at least once per week, the author reflects upon aspects of 1950's life, bygone industries, landmarks and some of the local characters that made Hindpool one of Barrow's most fascinating places in which to belong.

Paperback: 140 pages
Publisher: Stanley Henderson
Language: English
ISBN-13: 978-1916021747

available at amazon

Paperback: 84 pages
Publisher: Stanley Henderson
Language: English
ISBN-13: 978-1916275836

available at amazon

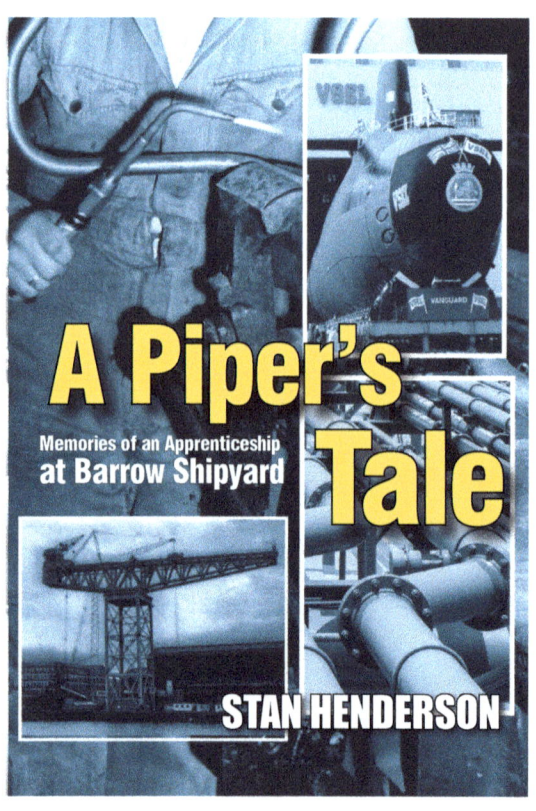

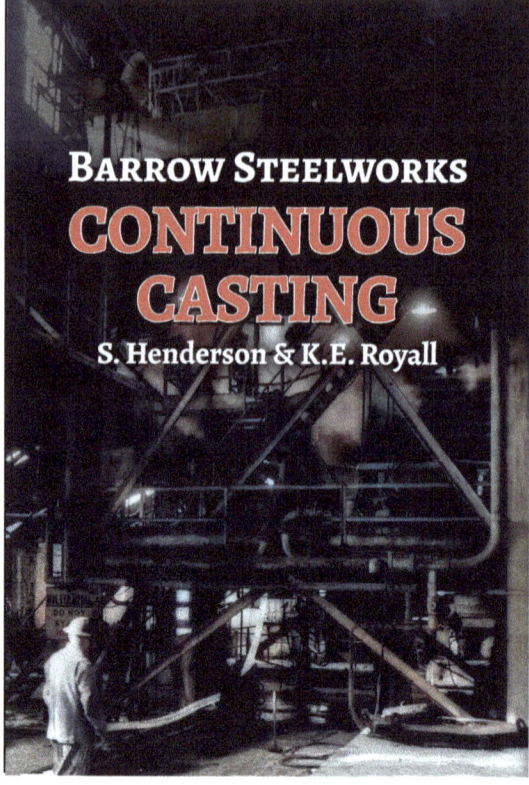

A Pipers Tale records the impressions made on a teenager as he makes his way into the thorny world of shipbuilding. A world in which the author, during the 1960s, witnessed the change from traditional shipbuilding, where vessels were constructed with a minimum, but adequate, level of technical support via long established trade practices and skills, to the cutting-edge of science-based projects as the Yard at Barrow became a 'Leader in Marine Technology' with the making of sophisticated warships and first-of-class vessels. Saluting the the wealth of characters and personalities that comprised the Yard's Plumbing Fraternity.

Paperback: 96 pages
Publisher: Stanley Henderson
Language: English
ISBN-13: 978-0995619081

available at amazon

Since the end of the Second World War (1939-1945), there have been some outstanding technical developments in steelmaking, which have since been adopted on a worldwide basis. These developments include the use of oxygen in bulk; automation; high-speed rolling and continuous casting. During the 50s & 60s, the works at Barrow adopted all four initiatives in varying degrees. Most notable for us was the development of High-Speed Continuous Casting. In this book the authors are attempting to lay down a permanent record of what was achieved locally and thereby, hopefully, preserving the memory of a once-proud industry.

Paperback: 88 pages
Publisher: Stanley Henderson
Language: English
ISBN-13: 978-1913898243

available at amazon

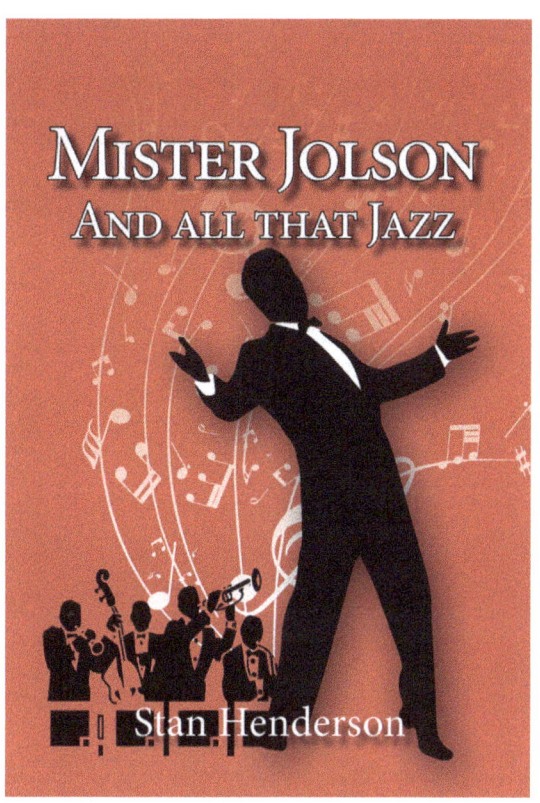

In this book, which is an appreciation of the popular art, the author takes us on a fleeting excursion through the evolution of 'pop' - from ragtime to hot jazz and in to the swing era - a fascinating insight into the early Broadway Musical and the birth of the 'talkies'.

The emergence of the Great American Song Book, and the influence of Al Jolson's career on popular singing; his relationship with the principal song writers, and how he inspired the great vocal stars who followed, including Ethel Waters, Bing Crosby, Judy Garland and Frank Sinatra.

Paperback: 92 pages
Publisher: Stanley Henderson
Language: English
ISBN-13: 978-1913898045

www.ingramcontent.com/pod-product-compliance
Lightning Source LLC
Chambersburg PA
CBHW051318110526
44590CB00031B/4395